THE MESSY LOT

Written by Larry Dane Brimner

Illustrated by Christine Tripp

THE CORNER KIDS

Children's Press®
A Division of Scholastic Inc.
New York • Toronto • London • Auckland • Sydney
Mexico City • New Delhi • Hong Kong
Danbury, Connecticut

For Haley McClure
—L.D.B.

For my husband Don
—C.T.

Reading Consultants
Linda Cornwell
Coordinator of School Quality and Professional Improvement
(Indiana State Teachers Association)

Katharine A. Kane
Education Consultant
(Retired, San Diego County Office of Education and San Diego State University)

Visit Children's Press® on the Internet at:
http://publishing.grolier.com

Library of Congress Cataloging-in-Publication Data

Brimner, Larry Dane.
   The messy lot / by Larry Dane Brimner ; illustrated by Christine Tripp.
      p. cm. — (rookie choices)
   Summary: When the Corner Kids decide to clean up a dump to make it a playground,
Alex's bossy ways hamper their progress.
   ISBN 0-516-22156-6 (lib. bdg.)   0-516-25975-X (pbk.)
   [1. Bossiness—Fiction. 2. Litter (Trash)—Fiction.] I. Tripp, Christine, ill. II. Title.
III. Series.
PZ7.B767 Mg 2001
[E]—dc21
                                                    00-047371

GROLIER
PUBLISHING

3 4 5 6 7 8 9 10 R 10 09 08 07 06 05 04 03 02

This book is about

cooperation.

"This place could be a neat playground," said Three J.

"Look around," said Gabby. "It's a dump!"

There were tires.

There was a refrigerator.

There were papers and bottles
and even somebody's dead
Christmas tree.

"It's not supposed to be a dump,"
said Alex. "We could clean it up."

"We could plant some trees,"
said Three J. "We could make
a playground."

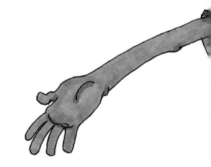

10

Gabby, Alex, and Three J called themselves the Corner Kids. They collected supplies and met at the lot.

"I made a list of things we need to do," Alex said. He sounded very important.

"Three J, stack up those tires," Alex said. "Then go to Lester's Fix-It Shop and ask Lester if he will haul them away in his truck. Oh, and do something about that refrigerator."

"But…" said Three J.

"Not now," said Alex. "We have too much to do." He looked at his list.

"Okay, Gabby, get those bottles and papers ready to recycle," he said.

Three J started stacking tires at the curb. Gabby started putting bottles and papers into piles.

Alex watched them work.

In a short while, Gabby and Three J took a break. Alex clapped his hands.

"Keep working," he said. "We still have a lot to do."

Three J and Gabby looked at each other.

"That does it," said Three J.

"It's all yours, Alex," said Gabby.

They dropped their gloves
and marched across the street.
They rested in the cool shade.

What's wrong with them?
Alex wondered.

Then he looked around at the neat
piles and tidy stacks, and he knew.

Alex crossed the street, too.

"I'm sorry," he said. "I wasn't much help. I'll help now."

In no time, *all* the Corner Kids
were back at work.

Then the grown-ups came. Lester, Alex's mom, and Three J's stepmom and dad all pitched in to help. So did Gabby's mom, dad, and grandmother.

Everyone was working,
and laughing, together.

Who needed a boss!

ABOUT THE AUTHOR

Larry Dane Brimner studied literature and writing at San Diego State University and taught school for twenty years. The author of more than seventy-five books for children, many of them Children's Press titles, he enjoys meeting young readers and writers when he isn't at his computer.

ABOUT THE ILLUSTRATOR

Christine Tripp lives in Ottawa, Canada, with her husband Don; four grown children—Elizabeth, Erin, Emily, and Eric; son-in-law Jason; grandsons Brandon and Kobe; four cats; and one very large, scruffy puppy named Jake.